Medicare's Private Parts

An Introduction To

Medicare Supplements

Medicare Part D

And

Medicare Advantage

Kelly James

Licensed

Health Insurance Agent

©2014 Integrated Senior Benefits LLC

Medicare's Private Parts An Introduction to Medicare Supplements, Medicare Part D And Medicare Advantage
ISBN-13:978 1499235708
ISBN-10: 1499235704
Non-Fiction Medicare Reference Book.

Introduction

When a person is transitioning into the Medicare eligible phase of their life, they may be faced with several decisions. These decisions have the potential to affect them financially. Most people enter this phase without the information they need to make the right choices. Many of them have no idea what's going on and they do what their friends or family members did, without examining their specific needs. Some do whatever their insurance agent tells them to do, which may not be a bad thing, provided that your agent knows what they're doing, and they have your best interests at heart.

At the time of writing this book, I have assisted hundreds Medicare beneficiaries in New York and New Jersey with their Medicare Plan selections. In doing so, I have had the privilege of serving people of all income types and with different coverage needs. I'm currently contracted with several of the largest insurance companies in the country, and I manage and train the agents in my organization on Medicare. While working with Medicare Beneficiaries, I noticed that there are far too many people out there that have no idea what they are getting into. And that's tragic because Medicare can be very simple if you take the time to do the research. I looked for books that I could recommend to my clients but I couldn't find a book that supplied people with pertinent information that was easy to digest, at least for someone without a health insurance license. A lot of the information is scattered and a lot of it's unclear. So I decided to write one myself.

I wanted this book to be easy to understand, as well as concise, and provide enough information for you to make the right decisions on your coverage. In this book, I'll walk you through Medicare Parts A and B, and then introduce you to the private parts of Medicare. And by private parts I mean the parts of Medicare that are offered by private insurance companies like, Medicare Supplements, Medicare Part D and Medicare Advantage. I have always felt that with the right information a person can make their own decisions, so I tried my best not to offer any advice and only give you the facts. Use this book as a reference for information on the workings of the private plans available for Medicare. You might not find every ounce of information available on Medicare in this book, so I suggest that you contact Medicare directly, and contact the private insurers that offer the Medicare plans that you might be interested in so that you can gather as much information as possible. Consider this to be a place for you to start. Hopefully, it helps you to ask the right questions so that you can get all the facts you need to make your decision. The information provided in this book is based on the 2014 plan year. Medicare cost and coverage are subject to change on a yearly basis, so if you get your hands on this book after 2014, contact Medicare directly for up to date information on Medicare's coverage.

This book was written with all of my clients in mind and with the knowledge that there are many other people who might have similar questions.

Table of Contents

Section 1: Original Medicare

Part 1

Medicare is a national social insurance program that is administered by the Centers for Medicare and Medicaid Services (CMS). Its purpose is to provide access to quality health care for Americans age 65 and over. Under Medicare, the financial risk of illness in this age group is spread across the American population, thus reducing individual risk. Medicare has two original parts; the card reads "Hospital Part A" and "Medical Part B". Part A is designed to help you with the cost of hospitalization and Part B is designed to help with the cost of outpatient and professional medical services.

Medicare Part A

Part A is the portion of Medicare that will help you with the cost of inpatient hospitalization. It will also help with the cost of skilled nursing facility care, hospice care, and home health care.

Medicare Part B

Part B generally covers outpatient care, services from doctors and/or Medicare approved health care providers like nurse practitioners, and physical therapists just to name a couple. Additionally, it assists with some preventative services, home health care coverage, and durable medical equipment, such as walkers, wheelchairs, oxygen tanks, and supplies for the tanks.

When Should I Apply?

Normally people get Medicare when they turn 65 years old, assuming they qualify. To qualify one must have paid Medicare taxes for ten years or forty quarters (four quarters per year- you get the idea). Another way to be eligible for Medicare is through disability. If someone is declared disabled by the federal government and entitled to social security disability income, they are normally automatically enrolled into Medicare Part A and B on the twenty-forth month of their active disability claim. No matter how old they are. There are also certain illnesses that trigger Medicare eligibility regardless of age. End Stage Renal Disease or ESRD, and Amyotrophic Lateral Sclerosis also known as Lou Gehrig's Disease automatically triggers eligibility for Medicare.

How Do I Enroll In Medicare?

A person with Lou Gehrig's Disease will get Part A and Part B automatically the month their disability benefits begin. A person diagnosed with ESRD will have to sign up for Medicare Part A and Part B by contacting Social Security. If you're receiving Social Security income benefits before your turn 65 years old, and you qualify for the Medicare program, you'll normally be automatically enrolled into Part A and Part B when you turn 65. You'll most likely receive your Medicare card in the mail and you'll be off to the races. If you're not receiving Social Security income benefits then you have to contact Social Security and request enrollment when you turn 65. If you call Medicare directly to apply they will tell you to call Social Security.

Enrollment Periods

There are specific times during the year when a person can enroll in Medicare. These times are based on a few factors or qualifying situations. These periods in time are known in the industry as enrollment periods. Enrollment periods are themselves very complicated, I have seen manuals over thirty pages long just about Enrollment Periods. So I'm going to do my best to break it down to the sections that you need to understand.

Remember getting hired for a new job, after the probation ended, if you had one, you were eligible to enroll into your job's group plan. Then if you chose not to enroll you had to wait until the next open enrollment period, or have a qualifying life event like getting married or having a baby to change, add, or drop coverage. It's very similar with Medicare. There are actually three types of Medicare enrollment periods, the initial enrollment period, the general enrollment period and special enrollment periods.

The Initial Enrollment Period - When a person is new to Medicare and approaching the normal Medicare age they have a period of time that is called the initial enrollment period. This is a seven month time span that starts three months before the month of your 65th birthday, the month of your 65th birthday and three months after, for a total of seven months. If you enroll during the first three months of your Initial Enrollment Period, your coverage will start on the first day of the month of your 65th birthday, unless your birthday is the first of the month, in which case your Medicare coverage will start on the first day of the month before. If you enroll during any one of the three months after the month of your 65th birthday then your coverage may be delayed. In my experience, people who enroll in Medicare during the last three months of their Initial Enrollment Period are more often than not retro actively enrolled as of the first day of the month of their 65th birthday anyway. If you choose not to enroll during this Initial Enrollment Period, or even if you forget, and you don't have any creditable coverage, you will have to wait until the general enrollment period to enroll. This choice or oversight may come with penalties.

The General Enrollment Period- Every year people who are Medicare eligible, but missed their initial enrollment period have the opportunity to sign up for Medicare during a three month span of time known as the general enrollment period. It begins on January 1st and ends on March 31st. If you enroll during this time your coverage will begin on July 1st of that year. You may however have to pay higher premiums for Medicare Part A and/or Part B for late enrollment.

The Special Enrollment Period- If you were Medicare eligible and did not enroll when you were first eligible because you were covered by a group health plan based on current employment, whether it was your own, a spouse's, or a family member's if you're disabled, you can sign up for Medicare Part A and/or B:

- At anytime while you're still covered by the group plan

- During the 8 month period that starts the month after your employment or coverage ends, whichever happens first.

Normally people who sign up during the special enrollment period don't have to pay a late enrollment penalty. The ppecial enrollment period doesn't apply to people with End Stage Renal Disease ESRD. You may also qualify for a special enrollment period if you were in another country volunteering during your initial enrollment period. COBRA coverage and retiree group health plans aren't considered coverage based on current employment, so please keep in mind that if you're currently covered under those plans you will not get a Special Enrollment Period when that coverage ends.

Do I Need Medicare?

Most private insurance companies will not cover people age 65 and over unless they are part of a group plan. And the reason is obviously that people in that age group have a higher risk of getting sick, the kind of sick that would cost a private insurance company a lot of money. Medicare's purpose is to spread the financial risk of illness in this age group across the entire nation, thus limiting the financial hardship that an illness can cause any one person. If you do not have a health plan from your employer, union, or your spouse or family member's employer or union, it will be extremely difficult to find an individual health plan that will give you health coverage without Medicare. And if you did, good luck trying to pay those premiums. So the short answer is yes, if you're Medicare eligible and not currently covered by a group health plan, I would recommend that you take Medicare.

If you become Medicare eligible and you're still working, or if you're covered under your spouse's group health plan from their employer or union, your best bet is to contact your employer or union's benefits coordinator to find out how your coverage would work with Medicare. In some cases you might not need to take Medicare Part A or B as long as you remain employed. It's important that you check with your benefits coordinator before you sign up for Medicare, because it might benefit you to delay your Medicare enrollment. Don't worry you can enroll into Medicare at any time during the employment or up to 8 months after the employment or the coverage ends, if the need arises.

COBRA

If you currently have COBRA, you shouldn't wait until the COBRA ends to sign up for Medicare Part B. You'll regret it, COBRA coverage is not considered coverage based on employment. So if you choose to wait until your COBRA coverage ends and you miss your Initial Enrollment Period then you will have to wait until the General Enrollment Period, and you could be subject to the penalty.

Retiree Health Plans

Retiree health plans are not considered coverage based on employment. Now this one is tricky because retiree health plans come in a lot of different flavors, but here's the bottom line. If you are approaching your initial enrollment period, and you are currently a member of a retiree health plan consult with your benefits coordinator early to find out if/how your plan works with Medicare. Some retiree health plans expect you to take Medicare when you are eligible so the coverage ends, some require you to enroll in Medicare and based on the plan and a few other factors, Medicare will be the primary or the secondary payer. The key here is to check with your benefits coordinator.

Part 2: How Much Does It Cost?

Most people do not pay for Medicare Part A, however most people will pay for Medicare Part B. Generally, if you or your spouse paid Medicare taxes while working for ten years or forty quarters, you will not have to pay for Medicare Part A. This is sometimes called "premium free Part A". This is why you have to contact the Social Security Administration (SSA) to apply for Medicare, they keep a tally of all of your income tax credits and they determine if you have to pay for Medicare Part A. In 2014, if you do not qualify for premium free Part A and you choose to buy Medicare Part A, the monthly premium is $426. Generally, if you chose to buy Part A you must also have Part B and pay the monthly premiums for both.

Most people will pay for Medicare Part B. How much you pay will be based on your income level. Below is a chart that outlines what you pay for Medicare Part B based on your income level.

Medicare Part B premiums based on income			
If you file an individual tax return	If you file a joint tax return	If your file married and separate tax return	Monthly Premiums in 2014
$85,000 or less	$170,000 or less	$85,000 or less	$104.90
$85,000 to $107,000	$170,000 to $214,000	N/A	$146.90
$107,000 to $160,000	$214,000 to $320,000	N/A	$209.80
$160,000 to $214,000	$320,000 to $428,000	$85,000 to $129,000	$272.70
$214,000 and up	$428,000 and up	$129,000 and up	$335.70

Late Enrollment Penalties

Part A

If you are not eligible for premium free Part A, and you don't buy it during your Initial Enrollment Period, your monthly premium may increase by 10%. You will pay the higher premium for twice the number of years that you could have had Part A, but chose not to take it.

Part B

If you don't enroll into Part B during your Initial Enrollment Period, you may have to pay a late enrollment penalty for as long as you have Part B. The penalty is 10% for each full 12 month period that you were eligible for Part B but elected not to sign up. However if you qualify for a Special Enrollment Period as mentioned previously, you can usually avoid the penalty.

Paying Medicare Premiums

People who receive Social Security, Railroad Retirement Board benefits, or Office of Personnel Management benefits will get their Part B premiums deducted from their monthly benefit payments automatically. If you don't receive these benefit payments and you chose to buy Part B, then you will receive a bill. If you have to pay for Medicare Part A, you'll always get a bill for the premium.

Medicaid

Some Medicare beneficiaries are eligible for both Medicare and Medicaid based on their income level. In the industry this is referred to as dual eligible. In this case Medicaid would pay your Medicare premiums, and in some cases even help you with some or all of your out of pocket costs (deductibles, copayments and coinsurance). For more information on Medicaid availability in your state contact your local Medicaid office or you can contact Medicare.

Part 3: What Does Medicare Cover?

Medicare Part A

Medicare Part A helps to cover inpatient hospital stays, skilled nursing facility stays, home health care, inpatient mental health, hospice care, blood, and inpatient care in a religious non-medical healthcare institution. It will cover a semi private room, meals, general nursing and prescription drugs while you are hospitalized.

Inpatient Hospitalization

The Deductible- Under Medicare Part A once you are formally admitted to the hospital there is a deductible that must be paid. In 2014, the deductible is $1,216. Keep in mind that the hospital will bill you for the deductible, they won't come to your bedside and ask you for a check. Medicare will cover the first sixty days of a hospital stay less the deductible. This next bit is important, and a lot of people don't even realize it. The Part A deductible isn't like a normal yearly deductible. It's payable every sixty days. For example: Let's say on January 5th, Sally was admitted to the hospital and stays two weeks. She would be responsible for the deductible of $1,216 and Medicare Part A would cover the rest. She's seemingly healthy for the next ninety days, then suddenly falls ill, and is admitted to the hospital again, keep in mind it's within the same year. Sally would be responsible for the $1,216 deductible again because it has been more than sixty days and the Part A benefit period is sixty days.

Copayments- For a continuous stay past sixty days, days 61 to 90 to be exact there is a co-pay of $304 per day, then for days 91 to 150 the co-pay becomes $608 per day, for days 151 and beyond you're on your own.

Lifetime Reserve Days- Days 91 to 150 are special, they are called lifetime reserve days, and you only get them once per lifetime. Let's

9

say our friend Sally spends 150 days in the hospital this year, then ten years later she has to be admitted again, at this point Medicare will only cover days 1 to 90 less the deductible, and co-pays listed above because she already used all of her lifetime reserve days which start after day 90 and only cover you up to 60 days. So in that case, after day 90, if she has no other coverage, she would be on her own.

Skilled Nursing Facility

Part A helps to cover semi-private rooms, meals, skilled nursing services, rehabilitation and other medically necessary services and supplies after a minimum of 3 days spent in the hospital as an inpatient for a related illness or injury. Inpatient hospital stays begin the day you're formally admitted by a doctor and don't include the day you are discharged. You pay nothing for days 1 to 20 if you are admitted to a skilled nursing facility. Days 21 to 100 will cost you $152 per day. Beyond day 100, you're on your own.

Hospice Care

Generally you pay nothing for hospice care with some exceptions. You may need to pay a little for prescription drugs but if you do, it won't be more than a $5 copayment. You may also have to pay 5% of the Medicare approved amount for respite care. In addition Medicare doesn't cover room and board when for hospice care in your home or another facility where you live, for example a nursing home.

Home Health Care

Medicare will cover part time or intermittent skilled nursing care, physical therapy, speech-language pathology services, and/or occupational therapy. You must be seen in person by a doctor or a health care provider who works with a doctor who can certify that it is medically necessary for you to receive this type of care. Home health care must be ordered by a doctor, and it must be provided by a

Medicare-certified home health care agency. Home health care might also include medical social services, home health aide services both part-time and intermittent and medical supplies for use at home. In order for Medicare to cover home health care you must be homebound. To be considered homebound, you must meet both of the following criteria: You are not able to leave home without considerable and taxing effort; and due to illness or injury leaving home isn't medically advisable or isn't possible without the aid of support devices, use of special transportation, or the assistance of another person.

Home health care services cost you nothing. Durable medical equipment associated with home health care will cost you 20% of the Medicare-approved cost.

Inpatient Mental Health

For inpatient mental healthcare the cost sharing is similar to that of a regular hospital stay. Furthermore you pay 20% of the Medicare-approved amount for the services you receive from doctors and other providers while you're an inpatient in the hospital. And finally, there is a lifetime limit of 190 days for inpatient mental healthcare.

Blood

If your hospital gets blood from a blood bank at no cost then you will not have to pay for it, but if the hospital has to buy the blood for you then you have to pay the hospital's cost for the first 3 units that you get in a calendar year.

Inpatient Care In A Religious Non-Medical Healthcare Institution

If your religious beliefs prohibit conventional medical care, and you qualify for hospital or skilled nursing facility care, Medicare will only cover the non medical items and services that you receive in a religious non-medical health care institution. For example room and board or any services that don't require a doctor's prescription like a simple walker or unmedicated wound dressings.

Medicare Part B

Medicare Part B helps to cover doctors' services, outpatient care, home health care, preventive services, and durable medical equipment. Doctors services can include both inpatient and outpatient doctor services. Most people think that if they are admitted to the hospital then Part A will cover everything. That isn't always true, Part B can cover doctors' services in and out of the hospital. A service provider must accept Medicare assignment, which basically means that the medical professional agrees to Medicare's fee schedule. If not you could end up paying for the service on your own. Medicare-approved service providers can be nurse practitioners, physical therapist and even social workers.

The Deductible - In 2014 the annual deductible is $147.

Coinsurance – After the deductible you pay 20% of the Medicare-approved amount for most doctor, and Medicare-approved medical professionals, and outpatient services.

Outpatient Care

Outpatient care refers to the care you receive from doctors and other Medicare-approved service providers on an outpatient basis. This type of care is subject to the Part B deductible, once the deductible is met you would be responsible for 20% of the Medicare approved cost of the service. Again, the service must be received from a doctor or service provider who accepts assignment.

Preventive Services

A preventative service is any health care service intended to prevent or detect an illness it at an early stage, because that's when treatment is likely to be more effective, such as flu shots or mammograms. Under Part B you pay nothing for most covered preventative services, as long as you get the service from a provider who accepts assignment. However you may have to pay a deductible, coinsurance or both for some preventative services. For a list of covered preventative services please visit www.medicare.gov or you may call Medicare at 1-800-Medicare.

Durable Medical Equipment

Part B covers items like wheel chairs, hospital beds, oxygen tanks and supplies for in home use, I've even seen Part B cover a motorized scooter. The important thing to remember however is that before Medicare will cover these items they must be ordered by a doctor or a Medicare-approved medical provider, and you must get them from Medicare contracted suppliers. There are several items that are considered durable medical equipment, for a list of these items and a list of Medicare contracted suppliers you can call 1-800-Medicare or visit Medicare's website www.medicare.gov.

Additional Notes About Medicare Part A and B

Hospitalization- You are considered an outpatient until you are formally admitted to the hospital. If you spend the night at the hospital and you are not formally admitted, you will be covered under Part B and subject to the Part B deductible and coinsurance. Imagine for a moment that Steve walks into the emergency room at 9:00 PM. He spends about three hours waiting for care, then finally sees a doctor who orders an array of lab tests. Steve then waits for another three hours before they perform the tests and waits an additional three hours for the results. After receiving the results, he waits for two hours before being released with a clean bill of health. During this time, he was not formally admitted, however, Steve did spend the night in the hospital. Part A would not cover his stay. Remember, Part A will only cover you if you are formally admitted, if not, you will be covered by Medicare Part B and subject to the Part B deductible and coinsurance.

Drugs- Part B will also cover drugs under special conditions. Generally, the Part B covered drugs are the types of drugs you wouldn't give to yourself; the kind you'll get at the doctor's office, or at the hospital on an outpatient basis. For example, injectable osteoporosis drugs, known as Supartz injections or the drugs associated with chemotherapy (some chemotherapy drugs are now covered by Part D). Medicare Part B also covers some vaccinations, such as flu shots. With the exception of the types of drugs covered under Medicare Part B, Medicare doesn't normally not cover outpatient prescription drugs.

Cost Sharing- You are responsible for all deductibles, coinsurances and copayments, unless you have both Medicare and Medicaid, or you have another plan in place to help you with those costs. Those plans may be a group retiree health plan, a union plan, Medicare Advantage or a Medicare Supplement.

Part B- With the exception of most preventative services and screenings almost everything thing that is covered by Part B is subject to the deductible, after that you'll have to pay 20% of the Medicare approved amount.

Reminder- If you qualify for both Medicare and Medicaid, Medicare can potentially assist you with your cost sharing. Contact your local Medicaid office or call Medicare directly for more information.

What Doesn't Original Medicare Cover?

Original Medicare doesn't cover cosmetic surgery, routine dental, routine eye care, dentures, hearing aids, acupuncture, custodial care and long term care, and original Medicare doesn't cover outpatient prescription drugs.

For review the following chart will help you to visualize the out of pocket costs associated with Medicare.

2014 Out of Pocket Cost	
Medicare Part A premium	Most people pay $0 per month. If you have to pay for Part A it will cost you $426 per month.
Medicare Part A cost Sharing	-Deductible of $1,216 per benefit period - Days 61-90: $304 - Days 91-150 $608 (Lifetime reserve, up to 60 days past day 90 per lifetime) - After lifetime reserve days have been exhausted you pay all costs
Medicare Part B premium	Most people pay $104.90 per month
Medicare Part B cost sharing	- Deductible of $147 per year - After deductible you pay 20% of Medicare approved Part B costs.

Section 2: Medicare's Private Parts

The out of pocket costs associated with original Medicare Part A and B are known to the industry as "gaps" in Medicare's coverage. To help Medicare beneficiaries with those out of pocket costs additional options were created. These options are offered by private insurance companies. Medicare's private parts come in following categories:

- Programs that work with Medicare that have to be contracted directly with Medicare
- Programs that work with Medicare that are completely private and are not contracted with Medicare but must however adhere to specific guidelines.

Part 1A: Non-Subsidized Private Offerings

Medicare Supplements (Medigap)

Medicare Supplements are private health insurance plans that work with Medicare. When you purchase a Medigap policy you are buying insurance that picks up all, most, or some of the cost sharing (deductibles, copayments and coinsurances) that Medicare doesn't cover. With Medigap, when you go to the doctor you present your original Medicare card and the Medigap insurance card. Medicare will pay its portion of the Medicare-approved service and the Medigap plan will pay its share.

Open Enrollment Period: The Best Time To Buy Medigap

In many states the Open Enrollment Period starts the first day of the month that you turn 65 or older and you are enrolled in Medicare Part B (you must also have Medicare Part A), and it continues for 6 months. During this time the insurer can't use medical underwriting. Therefore the insurance company can't:

- Decline you based on health issues

- Charge you a higher premium based on health issues

- Postpone your coverage based on health issues*

IMPORTANT!

The insurance company may be able to postpone your coverage if it pertains to a pre-existing condition. A pre-existing condition is a health issue you had before the start date of your new coverage. In some cases an insurer can refuse to cover your out of pocket costs for a pre-existing condition for up to 6 months. It's known in the industry as a "pre-existing condition waiting period." After 6 months the policy will cover the out of pocket cost associated with the pre-existing condition.

The coverage of a pre-existing condition can only be refused if the condition was diagnosed or treated within 6 months before the start date of the plan. This is known as the "look-back period."

If you are purchasing a Medigap plan to replace coverage that is considered "creditable coverage" you may be able to avoid or reduce the pre-existing condition waiting period. If you had at least 6 months of continuous creditable coverage, with no break in coverage for more that 63 days before the start of your Medigap policy, the insurer can't refuse to cover your pre-existing conditions.

If you don't buy a Medigap plan when first eligible, there is no guarantee that the insurer will sell you the policy. If they do, they can charge you higher premiums for health conditions.

Employer/Union Coverage

If you postpone your Medicare Part B enrollment because you, your spouse, or a family member are still working and you are covered by a group health plan, you will be able to sign up for Part B at any time during the employment or during the 8 month period that starts when you stop working or when your coverage ends, whichever happens first. In this case, your Open Enrollment Period starts on the day your Part B starts and will continue for 6 months.

Guaranteed Issue Rights

The ideal time to purchase a Medigap policy is during your open enrollment period. However there are situations in which you have a guaranteed right to buy a Medigap policy. When you have guaranteed issue rights the insurer can't:

- Deny you Medigap coverage

- Refuse to cover pre-existing health conditions

- Charge higher premiums based on past or present health issues

While you have guaranteed issue rights you can purchase a Medicare supplement plan of your choice as long as it is sold in your home state (plan selection rules may apply). For more information on guaranteed issue rights contact your Medigap insurer or call Medicare directly. You have guaranteed issue rights if:

- Your Medicare Advantage Plan lost its Medicare contract, is leaving your service area, or you move outside of the plans service area.

- You have Original Medicare Part A and B and an employer group health plan (includes retiree COBRA), or union coverage that pays after Medicare, and that plan is ending. (you may have additional options under state law).

- You have Original Medicare and a Medicare SELECT policy and you move out of the plan's service area.

- You signed up for a Medicare Advantage Plan or Programs of All-inclusive Care for the Elderly (PACE) during your Initial Enrollment Period and in the first year of coverage you decide to switch to Original Medicare (this is called a trial right).

- You canceled Medigap coverage to join a Medicare Advantage or a Medicare SELECT plan for the first time, you had the plan for less than a year and you decide to switch back (This is also called a trial right).

- Your Medigap insurer goes out of business or you lose coverage through no fault of your own.

- You cancel a Medigap or a Medicare Advantage policy because the company didn't follow rules or you were misled.

Note: Be sure to hold on to any letters you receive from your health insurance company; some guaranteed issue rights start as of the date on the notice that you are losing coverage.

Medicare Supplements Are Standardized

In most states Medicare Supplements are standardized by federal law. They are designated by letters A through N. The difference between them is how much of Medicare's gaps they cover. In general the higher the monthly premium the more coverage over and above original Medicare you will receive. Currently Medigap plans do not cover outpatient prescription drugs, but they can assist with the cost of the Part B drugs we discussed previously. The following chart displays the different Medigap coverage options and what they cover.

Benefits	Medicare Supplement Plans									
	A	B	C	D	F*	G	K**	L**	M	N
Part A Deductible		100%	100%	100%	100%	100%	50%	75%	50%	100%
Part A coinsurance and hospital cost up to an additional 365 days after Medicare benefits are used	100%	100%	100%	100%	100%	100%	100%	100%	100%	100%
Part A hospice care coinsurance and/or copayment	100%	100%	100%	100%	100%	100%	50%	75%	100%	100%
Part B deductible			100%		100%					
Part B coinsurance or copayments	100%	100%	100%	100%	100%	100%	50%	75%	100%	100% ***
Part B excess charges					100%	100%				
Skilled nursing facility coinsurance			100%	100%	100%	100%	50%	75%	100%	
Blood First 3 units	100%	100%	100%	100%	100%	100%	50%	75%	100%	100%
Foreign travel emergency coverage (up to plan limit)			100%	100%	100%	100%			100%	100%
2014 out of pocket Limit	Only applies to plan K and L						$4,940	$2,470		

There is also a high deductible F or F+ plan available in select states. If you choose an F+ plan, you must pay all of your Medicare deductibles, coinsurances, and copayments up to the deductible before the policy starts to pay. In 2014 the deductible is $2,140.

**Plans K and L have out of pocket limits. Once you pay your Part B deductible ($147 in 2014) and you reach the out of pocket limit, the plan pays 100% of covered services for the rest of the calendar year.

*** Plan N pays 100% or Part B coinsurance, minus a copayment of up to $20 for some doctor visits and up to $50 copayment for emergency room visits if they don't end in inpatient admission.

Part B Excess Charges

Some providers are allowed to charge 15% above Medicare's-approved amounts for their service. This is known as the Part B excess charge.

With the exception of Massachusetts, Minnesota and Wisconsin, insurance companies that offer Medigap policies can only sell standardized policies so they must have certain benefits. In general all the plans will give you the same coverage, the only difference from one company to the next will be the cost.

Plan Availability

Medigap insurers don't have to offer every supplement plan. But they must offer Plan A if they intend to offer any at all. If they want to offer another plan in addition to Plan A, they must offer Plan C or F. As long as they follow those rules, they can select the plans they want to offer. However state laws may affect plan offerings.

Important- Federal Law doesn't require insurance companies to sell Medigap plans to people under 65 years old. So if you have Medicare as a result of a disability or End-Stage Renal Disease (ESRD) you may not be able to purchase a Medigap policy. However, some states do require insurers to sell Medigap policies to people under 65. At the time this book was written, the following states required Medigap insurers to offer at least one type of Medigap policy to Medicare Beneficiaries under 65.

California	Maine	New York
Colorado	Maryland	North Carolina
Connecticut	Massachusetts	Oklahoma
Delaware	Michigan	Oregon
Florida	Minnesota	Pennsylvania
Georgia	Mississippi	South Dakota
Hawaii	Missouri	Tennessee
Illinois	Montana	Texas
Kansas	New Hampshire	Vermont
Louisiana	New Jersey	Wisconsin

Note: If you live in a state that requires Medigap insurers to offer Medigap plans to Medicare beneficiaries under 65, check with your state insurance department because additional conditions may apply.

What Medigap Doesn't Cover

Normally, Medigap doesn't cover long term care (nursing home), vision dental, hearing aids, eyeglasses, or private duty nursing.

Part 1B: Massachusetts, Minnesota, and Wisconsin Medigap Plans

Massachusetts Medigap Benefits

• Covers the Part A coinsurance plus an additional 365 days after Medicare coverage ends

• Covers the Part B coinsurance (normally 20% of Medicare-approved amount)

• Covers the first 3 units of blood each year

• The Part A hospice coinsurance or copayment

"X" means coverage

Benefits	Core Plan	Supplement Plan 1
Basic Benefits	X	X
Part A inpatient hospitalization deductible		X
Part A skilled nursing facility coinsurance		X
Part B deductible		X
worldwide emergency		X
Inpatient mental health	60 days/calender year	120 days/benefit year
State required benefits Include annual Pap tests, mammograms etc. (Check plan benefit summary for other state mandated benefits.)	X	X

Minnesota Medigap Benefits

• Covers Part A coinsurance (inpatient hospitalization)

• Part B Coinsurance (normally 20% of Medicare-approved amount)

• The first 3 units of blood

• Hospice and respite cost sharing (Part A)

• Home health services and supplies cost sharing (Part A and B)

"X" means coverage

Plan benefits	Basic Plan	Extended Basic Plan
Basic Benefits	X	X
Part A Deductible		X
Part A skilled nursing facility coinsurance	X (100 days of SNF care)	X (120 days of SNF care)
Part B deductible		X
Worldwide emergency	80%	80%
Outpatient mental health	20%	20%
Usual and customary fees		80%
Medicare-approved Preventative care	X	X
Physical therapy	20%	20%
Coverage outside of the United States		80%
State required benefits (Includes diabetic equipment and supplies, routine cancer screening, reconstructive surgery and immunizations, check plan benefit summary for additional required services)	X	X

Note: Plan covers 100% after out of pocket maximum of $1,000 in calendar year.

Mandatory Riders

Insurers can offer 4 additional riders to the basic Plan. You can choose any one or all of them to suit your needs.

1. Part A Inpatient hospitalization deductible coverage

2. Part B deductible coverage

3. Usual and customary fees

4. Non-Medicare preventative services

Note: Special versions of Medigap Plans K, L, M, N and F+ are available.

Wisconsin Medigap Benefits

- Covers inpatient hospital coinsurance (Part A)

- Covers Part B coinsurance (normally 20%)

- Covers the first 3 units of blood

- covers Part A hospice coinsurance or copayment

"X" means coverage

Plan Benefits	Basic plan
Basic Benefits	X
Skilled nursing facility coinsurance (Part B)	X
Impatient mental health	175 days per lifetime in addition to Medicare's benefit
Home health care	40 visits in addition to Medicare's benefit
State mandated benefits (See plan benefit summary for details.)	X

Optional Riders

Medigap insurers are permitted to offer these 7 additional riders:

1. Part A deductible coverage

2. 50% Part A deductible

3. Part B deductible coverage

4. Part B copayment or coinsurance coverage

5. Part B excess charges

6. Additional home health care (365 visits including Medicare's benefit)

7. Worldwide emergency

Part 1C: Medicare Supplement Pricing

Medigap insurers can choose how they price their policies. Conventionally, Medigap policies can be priced or rated in three ways. These methods determine the monthly plan payments or premiums at the time you purchase the policy and how the rates change in the future. The following chart outlines all three methods and how they affect pricing.

Pricing Method	How price is determined	The break down
Community-rated (no-age)	Normally premiums are the same for everyone regardless of age	Not age based, but premium may increase based on inflation and other factors, but not age.
Issue age rating (entry-age)	Premium is based on how old you are when you initially buy the policy	Premiums are lowers for younger people at the time of purchase. They can increase due to inflation and other factors, but not age.
Attained age rated	Premiums are based on current age, therefore the premiums increase as you get older.	Premiums are lower for younger buyers. They eventually increase as you age. Premiums may also increase due to inflation and other factors.

From company to company premiums for Medigap polices may differ significantly, even for the same plan. As you shop for a plan, it's important that you ask the insurer how the plan is rated, and compare as many policies as you can. This way you are more likely to find the most cost effective option.

Medicare Select

In some states, Medigap insurers offer Medicare Select polices. These policies require you to use certain provider networks (except for emergencies). They can be in the form of any standardized plan design. Medicare select plans normally have lower monthly premiums. Be sure to check if your providers participate before you purchase these types of plans.

Part 2: Medicare Subsidized Private Offerings

Some Medicare plans are subsidized by Medicare. The federal government pays them money to make offering these products a little more palatable, and to alleviate the costs so that it is more affordable for the insurance company and the Medicare beneficiary. There are two types of Medicare subsidized private offerings:

1. Medicare Prescription Drug Plans (Part D)

2. Medicare Advantage (Part C).

Part 2A: Medicare Prescription Drug plans (Part D)

Part D is designed to help you with the cost of prescription drugs. Part D plans can only be offered by insurance companies that are contracted with Medicare and they must follow specific coverage guidelines. There are several factors involved when it comes to selecting a Part D plan or deciding not to select a plan at all. However, once you understand the rules and the coverage options, the choice should be relatively simple.

Election Periods

Similar to the enrollment periods of original Medicare, Part D has election periods. Election periods are times when you are allowed to enroll, change or disenroll from a Medicare Part D plan. The election periods are Initial Enrollment Period (IEP), Annual Election Period (AEP), Special Election Period (SEP), and the Annual Disenrollment Period. It is important to understand Election Periods because you need to have a valid Election Period in order to select a plan , otherwise you can't sign up.

Initial Election Period (IEP, IEP2)- This election period runs alongside original Medicare's initial enrollment period. It starts three months before the month of your 65th birthday, the month of your 65th birthday and three months after, for a total of seven months. During this time you are allowed to sign up for a Part D plan. If you were enrolled into Medicare prior to your 65th birthday (due to disability for example), and you already have a Part D plan, then during this time you can change your plan, this is referred to as IEP2 in the industry.

If you enroll during the first three months of your IEP then your Part D plan coverage will begin on the day that your Medicare is effective (Normally the first day of the month of your 65th birthday unless your birthday is the first day of the month, in which case your Medicare will be effective the first day of the month before). If you sign up during the month of, or at any time during the three months following your 65th birthday, your Part D coverage will begin on the first day of the month immediately after the signature date on your Part D enrollment form.

Annual Election Period (AEP)- The annual election period starts on October 15th of every year and ends on December 7th of the same year. During this time a Medicare beneficiary can sign up or change their Part D plan. If you sign up for a plan during this time your new plan will be effective on January 1st of the following year.

Medicare Advantage Annual Disenrollment Period- The annual disenrollment period takes place from January 1st to February 14th. People who signed up for Medicare Advantage Plans during AEP get the opportunity to change their mind and go back to Original Medicare and sign up for a standalone Part D plan. During the annual disenrollment period you can also buy a Medicare Supplement. If you sign up for a Part D plan during this time, your coverage will begin on the first day of the month following receipt of election.

Special Election Period (SEP)- Sometimes situations occur that trigger SEP's so that people can enroll, change or drop their Part D plan. Below is a list of the situations that can lead to an SEP.

- If you enrolled into Medicare Part B during the General Enrollment Period

- If you permanently move outside of your current plan's service area

- If you have both Medicare and Medicaid (Dual Eligible).

- If you have Extra Help or Low income Subsidy (LIS)

- If you lose either Medicaid or LIS status

- If you are institutionalized, meaning you live in a skilled nursing facility

- An involuntary loss of creditable coverage

- If your coverage is no longer considered creditable

- If you gain group coverage

- If your current Part D plan is non-renewing

- If your current plan's Medicare contract is terminated

- If you disenroll from a Medicare Advantage plan during the Annual Disenrollment Period

- If you enroll into a State Pharmacy Assistance Program (SPAP)

- If you are no longer eligible for a State Pharmacy Assistance Program

- If you are disenrolled from a Special Needs Plan because you are no longer eligible

- If you are disenrolled from the Program of All-inclusive Care for the Elderly (PACE)

- If you disenroll from a cost plan's optional supplemental Part D benefit, to get a Part D plan

- If you involuntarily lose Part B

If any of the above listed situations apply to you then you are entitled to an SEP. Contact Medicare or your Part D plan's customer service as soon as you are made aware of the circumstance, for details on your SEP, and instructions on how to enroll into the plan of your choice. Generally if you use an SEP to enroll into a Part D plan, your coverage will begin on the first day of the following month.

The Standard Part D Model of Coverage

Every Part D plan in the country no matter what insurance company you get it from has one thing in common, they all follow a specific model of coverage. This model sets forth a guideline that every Part D plan has to follow if they want to be contracted with Medicare. Each plan must offer at least as much coverage as the model dictates, they can offer more for additional premiums, but not less. People with low income and assets may qualify for state and/or federal subsidies that enhance their coverage, but the plan itself is still the same, the benefits are just bolstered by the additional subsidy that they are receiving. I give Medicare presentations about four to five times per week, almost every week, and this is the part that confuses people the most. So get comfortable and read carefully. The good news is once you get it, you wonder how it ever confused you in the first place, because it really isn't that bad.

To understand the Part D model of coverage you have to start with three basic facts. First, the Part D benefit period is a calendar year; second, it's based on the dollar amount that both you, and the insurance company spends on your prescription drugs (not including the premium); and third; all the drugs that the plan covers are organized into tiers based on the price and in some cases the drug type. Under Part D your coverage is divided into four stages:

- The Deductible Period

- The Initial Coverage Period

- The Coverage Gap

- Catastrophic Coverage

Let's take a look at each one individually. Please note that the coverage limits listed here are based on the 2014 model. The coverage limits and deductibles are subject to change yearly. If you are reading this book after 2014 please visit www.medicare.gov or you can call 1-800-Medicare for information on the current coverage limits.

The Deductible Period- This is the first period of the year. During this phase you pay the full cost of all your drugs until you reach the deductible. In 2014 the deductible is $310. Some plans eliminate the deductible period, for a higher premium of course, meaning that your prescriptions are covered from the first day of the year. In that case you would skip directly to the initial coverage period

The Initial Coverage Period- The initial coverage period starts once you hit the deductible. During this phase the insurance company steps in and pays its share of the cost of your prescriptions. You pay the copayments listed in the benefit summary of your plan based on the tier that each drug falls into. This will continue until the total cost of your prescriptions adds up to coverage limit. The deductible, all of your copayments, and coinsurances that you paid, plus whatever the insurance company paid for your drugs until that point are all counted towards the coverage limit. In 2014 the Part D initial coverage limit is $2,850.

The Coverage Gap- Also known as the "Donut hole" is reached when what you paid for your prescriptions (all copayments, coinsurances and even the deductible from the deductible period) plus what the insurance company paid to date, combined equals $2,850. During the Coverage Gap the insurance company will take a step back and you'll pay 72% of the cost of your generic drugs and 47.5% of the cost of your brand name drugs. The brand name drug manufacturers should contribute a 50% discount during this phase. This will continue until everything you have paid during the coverage gap, the initial coverage period, the deductible and any discounts that you may have received, plus whatever the insurance company paid in the initial coverage period and the coverage gap equals $4,550. So,this is essentially the entire cost of the all of your drugs up to that point.

The Catastrophic Coverage Period- Catastrophic Coverage is reached when what you have paid throughout the year, plus any discounts that you may have received, plus what the insurance company paid is combined for a total of $4,550. In this phase of coverage the insurance company comes back to pay the majority of the cost of your prescriptions. During the catastrophic coverage period you will pay $2.55 for generics, $6.35 for brand name or 5% coinsurance, whichever one is higher. This will continue for the rest of the year.

The following chart outlines the 4 stages of the Part D Model of coverage. Please note that these figures are based on the 2014 plan year and are subject to annual updates.

Deductible Period		
Annual Deductible $310		
Initial Coverage Period		
Plan pays 75%		Coinsurance 25% Most plans have copayments and coinsurance during this time.
Coverage Gap		
Plan pays 28% of generics and 2.5% for brand name drugs.	Drug manufacturer discount of 50% for brand name drugs.	Coinsurance of 72% for generics and 47.5% for brand name drugs.
Catastrophic Coverage		
Plan pays 95%		Copayment of 5% whichever is greater.

Part D Plan Formularies

A formulary is a fancy name for a list of covered drugs. This is important because although the formulary's guidelines are set by CMS, the insurance company still has the freedom to choose which drugs they will cover as long as their list complies with the regulations. The plan's list of drugs is developed by pharmacists, doctors and other experts. The difference from one Part D plan formulary to another can be devastating to your pocket. That's why it's important to check your prescriptions against the formulary of any plan you are interested in before you sign up. CMS mandates that a Part D formulary must:

- Include at least two drugs in each therapy category

- Include generic and brand-name drugs

Part D plans divide the formulary into tiers based on the cost of the drug. Each tier has a specific copayment. Plans usually have three to five tiers, for example:

- Tier 1: Generic drugs

- Tier 2: Preferred brand-name drugs

- Tier 3: Non-preferred brand name drugs

- Tier 4: Specialty or high cost drugs

Part D plans normally use tools to manage certain drugs, for example:

Step Therapy is when one or more similar, cheaper drugs must be tried before they cover the more expensive drugs.

Prior Authorization is when a doctor must contact the plan to prove that a drug is medically necessary before the plan will cover it.

By law Part D plans are not permitted to include the following:

- Drugs for weight loss or gain

- Fertility drugs

- Drugs for cosmetic purposes

- Symptomatic relief for cold and/or flu (For example, cough medicine)

- Vitamins

- Barbiturates (except when used for the treatment of cancer, epilepsy, or a chronic mental disorder)

- Erectile dysfunction drugs (When used for sexual dysfunction)

- Non-prescription drugs

- Part B covered drugs

Part D plans may offer supplemental benefits that can cover certain drugs that are not covered under Part D.

Important- All formulary changes must be approved by CMS. Insurers can't make formulary changes within the first 60 days of the calendar year, unless it's because a drug was removed from the market. After March 1st a plan may make some changes. You must be notified in advance before the changes. In some cases, if the change affects a drug you are currently taking, the plan must cover that drug for the rest of the year.

Premiums

Stand alone Part D plans normally have monthly premiums, they range from around $23 to roughly $110. Based on your income you might have to pay higher premiums for your Part D coverage. If so, the additional premium will be deducted from your Social Security benefits or billed by the Railroad Retirement Board if your receive RRB benefits. If you are billed by the RRB or Medicare you must pay them directly, do not send the payment to the Part D insurer.

Based on your income you may also be eligible for Extra Help our Low-Income Subsidy to help you with the cost of your premiums and out of pocket drug costs. It's important that you contact Social Security or Medicare to see if you qualify, even if you think your income might be too high because you never know.

Late Enrollment Penalty for Part D

In most cases, if you don't sign up for a Part D plan during your initial election period, and you don't have creditable prescription drug coverage for 63 consecutive days or more, after your IEP ends, you will be subject to the Part D late enrollment penalty.* This penalty is 1% or the national base Part D premium ($32.42 in 2014) for every month that you could have had Part D coverage but didn't have it. The amount is calculated and added to the monthly premium. The insurance company will inform you if you need to pay a penalty, and if you do you will have to pay it for as long as you have Part D.**

*If you receive Extra Help you will not have to pay the penalty.

**If you had Medicare before you turned 65, the penalty is normally waived once you turn 65.

Extra Help (Low Income Subsidy, LIS)

CMS offers a subsidy to Medicare beneficiaries with low incomes to help them with the cost of their prescription drugs. There are different levels of Extra Help, and if you qualify you can receive help with the cost of your Part D premiums and prescription co-pays and coinsurances. For information on Extra Help and to see if you qualify contact the Social Security Administration by visiting www.ssa.gov or call them directly at 1-(800) 772-1213, you can also contact Medicare by calling 1-800-Medicare or on the web at www.medicare.gov.

State Pharmaceutical Assistance Program (SPAP)

State Pharmaceutical Assistance Programs are programs that are administered by states for the purpose of assisting Medicare beneficiaries with the cost of prescription drugs. They are not available in every state but if your state has one, you may receive help with your Part D premiums, deductibles, co-pays and coinsurances, if you qualify. To find out if your state has a SPAP contact Medicare directly or visit www.medicare.gov. You can't get a SPAP if you already have extra help.

Think Co-Pays and Formularies First, Not Premiums

Personally I've seen Part D plans of all types with premiums ranging from $23 to over $100 per month. Some plans eliminate the deductible period so that your coverage starts from day one, some plans have more comprehensive formularies, and some plans even offer generic drug coverage with low co-pays during the coverage gap. When selecting a Part D plan, it's important that you take the time to examine your prescriptions and compare the cost and coverage of several plans. This way you can find the most cost effective solution. The lowest monthly premium is not always the best bet, take the time to do the homework. What should be important to you are the co-pays, coinsurances and the list of covered drugs rather than the monthly plan premiums. Now of course the monthly premium should be a factor, and it should play a role in your decision. However, sometimes a more expensive plan may have lower co-pays and have a more comprehensive formulary than a plan with a lower monthly premium. Therefore, over the course of a year your prescription drug expenses turn out to be less, even after you add the higher premium. I've seen it more than once. If you visit www.medicare.gov and use the plan finder you can actually input all of your drugs and it will tell you the plans in your area along with your drug costs for the year.

Part 2B: Medicare Advantage (Part C)

Medicare Advantage is private health insurance that is subsidized by Medicare. The insurance company must be contracted with Medicare to receive the subsidy, and the plan design must follow specific guidelines. These plans are normally county specific, so your friends and family in the next county over might have totally different benefits even though they have the same insurer. Medicare Advantage is extremely different from Medicare Supplements, in terms of premiums, and benefits. It's important for you to understand the differences before you make a decision on coverage.

How does Medicare Advantage work?

Part C is private health insurance that is subsidized by Medicare. These health plans do not work with Medicare Part A and Part B, instead they replace Part A and Part B. When you sign up for a Part C plan the contract that you signed is sent to CMS by the insurer, they verify the enrollment and they begin to pay the insurer on your behalf for the coverage as of the effective date on the application. In effect, Medicare is buying you your own health plan to use instead of Medicare. Keep in mind that if you sign up for a Part C plan, you will still be a member of Medicare, and you are still required to pay your Part A and/or B premium, however the Plan will pay your claims instead of Medicare, less any co-pays, coinsurances or deductibles. With a Part C plan you present your insurance card at the point of service or when you see the doctor, not your Medicare card because the insurance company pays the claim. At first, this is a point of confusion for many Medicare beneficiaries.

The question then becomes: How much does Medicare actually pay? The answer to that question is: It depends, the amount is county specific, all across the country. In the summer of 2013 I had lunch with a representative from one of the top three largest health insurance companies in the country. He told me that in the territory that I do business, Medicare pays about $1100 per month for Medicare Part C plans, per beneficiary, but again every county is different. The amount is subject to change on a yearly basis, which is one of the reasons that some Medicare Part C plan benefits also change yearly.

Election Periods

Very similar to Part D, Medicare Advantage plans have election periods. In order to enroll, change or drop Part C coverage, you must have a valid election period. The election periods are as follows:

Initial Election Period (IEP, IEP2)- The initial election period runs alongside Original Medicare's initial enrollment period. It starts three months before the month of your 65th birthday, the month of your 65th birthday and three months after, for a total of seven months. During this time, you are allowed to sign up for a Part C plan. If you were enrolled into Medicare prior to your 65th birthday (due to disability for example), and you already have a Part C plan, then during this time you can change your plan, this is referred to as IEP2.

If you enroll during the first three months of your IEP then your Part C plan coverage will begin on the day that your Medicare is effective (Normally the first day of the month of your 65th birthday unless your birthday is the first day of the month, in which case your Medicare will be effective the first day of the month before). If you sign up during the month of or at any time during the three months following your 65th birthday, your Part C coverage will begin on the first day of the month following the receipt of your election.

The Annual Election Period- The annual election period starts on October 15th of every year and ends on December 7th of the same year. During this time a Medicare beneficiary can sign up, change, or drop their Part C plan. If you sign up for a plan during this time your new coverage will be effective on January 1st of the following year.

The Special Election Period (SEP)- Similar to Part D, certain situations can trigger an SEP so that you can sign up for or change your Part C coverage. The following is a list of some of the most common situations that can lead to an SEP:

- If you signed up for Medicare Part B during the General Enrollment Period

- If you permanently move outside of your current plan's service area

- If you have both Medicare and Medicaid (Dual Eligible).

- If you have Low income Subsidy (LIS)

- If you lose either Medicaid or LIS status

- If you are institutionalized, meaning you live in a skilled nursing facility

- An involuntary loss of creditable coverage

- If your coverage is no longer considered creditable

- If your current Part C plan is non-renewing

- If your current plan's Medicare contract is terminated

- Retroactive Medicare Part B effective date

- If you enroll into a State Pharmacy Assistance Program (SPAP)

- If you are no longer eligible for a State Pharmacy Assistance Program

- If you are disenrolled from a Special Needs Plan because you are no longer eligible

- If you are disenrolled from the Program of All-inclusive Care for the Elderly (PACE)

- If you plan had a lower than 3 star rating for three consecutive years

- If there is a plan in your area with a 5 star rating

If any of the above listed situations apply to you then you are entitled to an SEP. Contact your Part C plan's customer service, or call 1-800-Medicare as soon as you are made aware of the circumstance for details on your SEP and instructions on how to enroll into the plan of your choice. Generally if you use an SEP to sign up for a plan your coverage will begin on the first day of the month following your election.

Benefits

Part C benefits are not standardized, but they must cover at least what original Medicare Part A and Part B covers. Many of them cover significantly more. Some Medicare Advantage plans include prescription drug coverage, so with one plan, and one insurance card, you can have all of your Medicare health benefits and your prescription drug benefits. Part C plans come in a few different varieties. They are as follows:

Health Maintenance Organization (HMO) – Medicare Advantage plans with doctor and hospital networks. Most HMO's require that you only get your care from doctors or hospitals in the plans network (except in emergencies). Many HMO plans do require you to select a Primary care physician, and get referrals before you see a specialist. Some HMO plans do not require a referral as long as the specialist is in the plans network, this is known in the industry as an open access HMO.

Health Maintenance Organization- Point-of-Service Plans (HMO-POS) – HMO-POS is a special kind of HMO in which you may receive care outside of the plans network under certain circumstances for a higher copayment or coinsurance. Many HMO plans do require you to select a Primary care physician, and get referrals before you see a specialist.

Preferred Provider Organization (PPO)– PPO plans have a network of doctors and hospitals, but if you are willing to pay a higher co-pay or coinsurance you can see a doctor outside of the network at any time.

Private Fee-For-Service (PFFS)– PFFS plans are plans that allow you to see any Medicare-approved doctor, hospital or any other provider that accepts the plan's payment terms and conditions as long as they agree to treat you. Some providers don't accept the terms and the ones that do may decide not to at any time. So if you select a PFFS plan make sure that you always check with the doctor to see if they accept the plan's terms before you receive service .

Special Needs Plans (SNP)– SNP plans have special benefit combinations for populations with special needs. For example: Dual eligible (Medicare and Medicaid), and people with chronic illnesses.

Medical Savings Account Plans (MSA) – MSA Plans combine high deductibles with a special savings account. The plan deposits money into the account for you to use until the deductible is reached.

Medicare Cost Plan– Cost plans allow you to see providers both in and out of the network. Medicare covered services will be covered by the plan when you see doctors in network. If you see a provider out of the network, Original Medicare will pay the claims but you will be responsible for all of Medicare's deductibles, copayments, and coinsurances.

Out of Pocket Limits

The entire purpose of health insurance is to protect you from potential financial loss due to illness or injury. So what's the point of having a health plan where you're subject to cost sharing without end. Out of pocket limits are there to cap your out of pocket costs, to further protect you from financial loss. Once you reach the out of pocket limit, you don't have to pay any more co-pays or coinsurance for the rest of the year. With Part C, generally HMO's have lower out of pocket limits than the other Part C plan options.

Premiums

What makes Part C plans so attractive for many Medicare beneficiaries is the cost. The monthly premiums are normally significantly less than many worthwhile Medigap plans, especially when you factor in the premiums of the Stand alone Part D plan that you will most likely need to buy. Part C plans in highly populated regions usually have lower premiums and richer benefits than less populated regions. So carefully look at the Part C benefits and premiums in your area to compare them to Medigap and Medicare Part D combinations.

Part C premiums vary from county to county. I've seen plan premiums from $0 per month to $213 per month and everything in between. These plans are normally not medically underwritten so when it comes to the price, there are several other factors involved. Pricing can be based on things like the Medicare subsidy amount, the performance of the plan in the county it serves, benefits, state and federal regulations, and contracts with provider networks.

Based on your income you might have to pay higher premiums for your Part C if your plan includes part D coverage. If so, the additional premium will be deducted from your Social Security benefits or billed by the Railroad Retirement Board, if your receive RRB benefits. If you are billed by the RRB or Medicare you must pay them directly, do not send the payment to the Part D insurer.

Based on your income you may also be eligible for Medicaid, or Low-Income Subsidy to help you with the cost of your premiums, and cost sharing. It's important that you contact Social Security or Medicare to see if you qualify, even if you think your income might be too high.

Out of Pocket Cost

Because of the tremendous variety of Part C plans and the variables that go into plan design, Part C plan benefits are difficult to sum up. However I can say that in general the HMO's tend to have lower premiums and cost sharing, or out of pocket costs. The trade off is that with HMO plans you are usually confined to a specific provider network. So, Part C plans won't fit everyone, but they are definitely worth consideration.

Who can get Medicare Part C?

To sign up for Part C you must:

• Have both Medicare Part A and B*

• Have a valid election period

*In general people with End Stage Renal Disease (ESRD) can't get Part C.

Conclusion: Make Your Selection Carefully

You can receive your Medicare coverage in a few ways using different coverage combinations. You can choose original Medicare, original Medicare with a Part D plan, original Medicare Part A and B with a Medigap policy and a Part D plan, or a Medicare Advantage plan that includes Part D. Your decision on how you receive your Medicare benefits will be based on whether or not you have retiree health benefits from your previous employer or union, whether or not you have Medicaid, and/or Extra Help, and your budget. The most important thing is that you investigate each option carefully, look at the coverage, the price, and the restrictions of each option. If your previous employer or union is offering retirement coverage, ask your benefit coordinator for detailed information on the plan so you can know what you have, and you can compare it to what's out there. You should also contact Medicare or Social Security to see what types of assistance are available in your area to help you with the cost or Medicare.

Sometimes the frequency of your doctor's visits can help you to determine which Medicare plan combination will work best for you. If you see specialists or you use outpatient services like chemotherapy multiple times per month, and you do not qualify for Medicaid, carefully review the plans in your area. Roughly estimate the cost of your monthly visits for each option. Many Part C plans might have $0 premiums, but have co-pays anywhere from $25 to $50 per visit for a specialist, and up to 20% for therapeutic radiology (chemotherapy). If you are using these services several times per month, it might be in your best interest to have a Medigap plan, You might end up saving money even with the higher monthly premiums. Do the math, and if need be consult with an agent licensed in your state, preferably one who represents several insurance carriers, that tends to keep us honest.

As I said in the introduction use the information in this book as a starting point. It wasn't intended to be your only source of information. I could write a book 400 pages long filled with all the information you will ever need on Medicare. But it's been my experience that people probably wouldn't read it. The people I meet every day as a health insurance agent, with a focus on Medicare, initially want fast easy to digest basic information. So, here it is, I hope it was helpful, and thank you for reading.

The information in this book is based on Medicare's 2014 coverage. If you're reading this book after 2014, please contact Medicare for up to date coverage information.

Definitions

Assignment: A doctor who accepts assignment agrees to be paid directly by Medicare. To accept the Medicare-approved payment amounts for service and they must not bill you for any more than the allowed Medicare deductible, coinsurance, and co-pays

Benefit Period: Begins the day you're admitted as an inpatient and ends when you haven't received inpatient care for 60 consecutive days.

Coinsurance: The amount that you pay for your share of covered medical services or supplies after your deductible. It is normally a percentage.

Copayment or Co-pay: The amount that you might have to pay for your share of approved medical service or supplies. It is normally a fixed dollar amount.

Cost Sharing: The share of your medical expenses that are your responsibility. Cost sharing can be in the form of coinsurance, co-pays, or deductibles, doesn't include premiums.

Creditable Prescription Drug Coverage: Prescription coverage from an employer or a union that is expected to pay at least as much as

Medicare's standard prescription drug coverage.

Custodial Care: Personal care provided by non skilled providers, for example help with bathing, dressing, eating, getting in or out of a chair or bed. In most cases, Medicare will not cover this kind of care.

Deductible: The amount that you must pay for health care prescriptions before your coverage begins.

Extra Help: A Medicare program to help people with the cost of prescription drugs, also called Low Income Subsidy.

Formulary: The list of drugs covered by a prescription drug plan.

Long Term Care: Medical and non medical care for people who are not able to perform basic activities of daily living.

Medically Necessary: Health care services of supplies needed to treat, prevent or diagnose illness or injury.

Medicare Approved Amount: The amount that a doctor or supplier who accepts assignment can be paid under original Medicare.

Premium: Monthly payments for original Medicare Part A and/or B, Part D, Medicare Advantage, or Medicare Supplement plans.

Primary Care Doctor: The doctor you normally see first. Some Medicare Advantage plans require you to select a primary care doctor.

Referral: Many HMO's require that you get this written order to see a specialist.

Service Area: The geographical health plan coverage area.

Skilled Nursing Facility (SNF): A facility where you receive care from skilled nurses on a continuous basis.

Important Contact Information

Social Security Administration (SSA)

Toll free: 1(800) 772-1213

on the web @ www.ssa.gov

Medicare

Toll free: 1-(800) Medicare (1-800-633-4227)

or on the web @ www.medicare.gov

www.ingramcontent.com/pod-product-compliance
Lightning Source LLC
Chambersburg PA
CBHW060647290526
45793CB00001B/439